# TIME, LOVE and LICORICE

Rosenberry
books,
etc.

WIPF & STOCK · Eugene, Oregon

# HOW TO USE THIS BOOK

*Time, Love and Licorice* is created to be a safe space in which children and families can face, process and try to heal from the disruptions caused by Post-Traumatic Stress Disorder (PTSD).

There are many ways that a child might helpfully approach this book, crayons in hand. While listening to the story, she may wish to color the decorative borders only, allowing the emotional story to process subconsciously while giving her conscious attention to coloring ordered patterns.

One child might discover that he and his family are missing from the pictures. This child may wish to draw himself into the pictures where another child may use his crayon to scribble emotional energy all over the page.

Coloring within the lines is not required here, unless that is what suits the personality of the child. The child's chosen method is the healing one, and if several copies of *Time, Love and Licorice* were available to the child, it may be found that his or her chosen method changes with time.

## For Aidan & Benjamin

Text copyright © 2015 by David H. Rosen.
Art copyright © 2015 by Diane Katz.

ISBN:

Designed by Rosenberry books, etc.
101 Nicks Bend West
Pittsboro, NC 27312
800.723.0336   919.969.2767
www.rosenberrybooks.com
Rosenberry books, etc. is a registered trademark.

Wipf & Stock is an imprint of Wipf and Stock Publishers.
199 W. 8th Ave., Suite 3
Eugene, OR 97401
wipfandstock.com

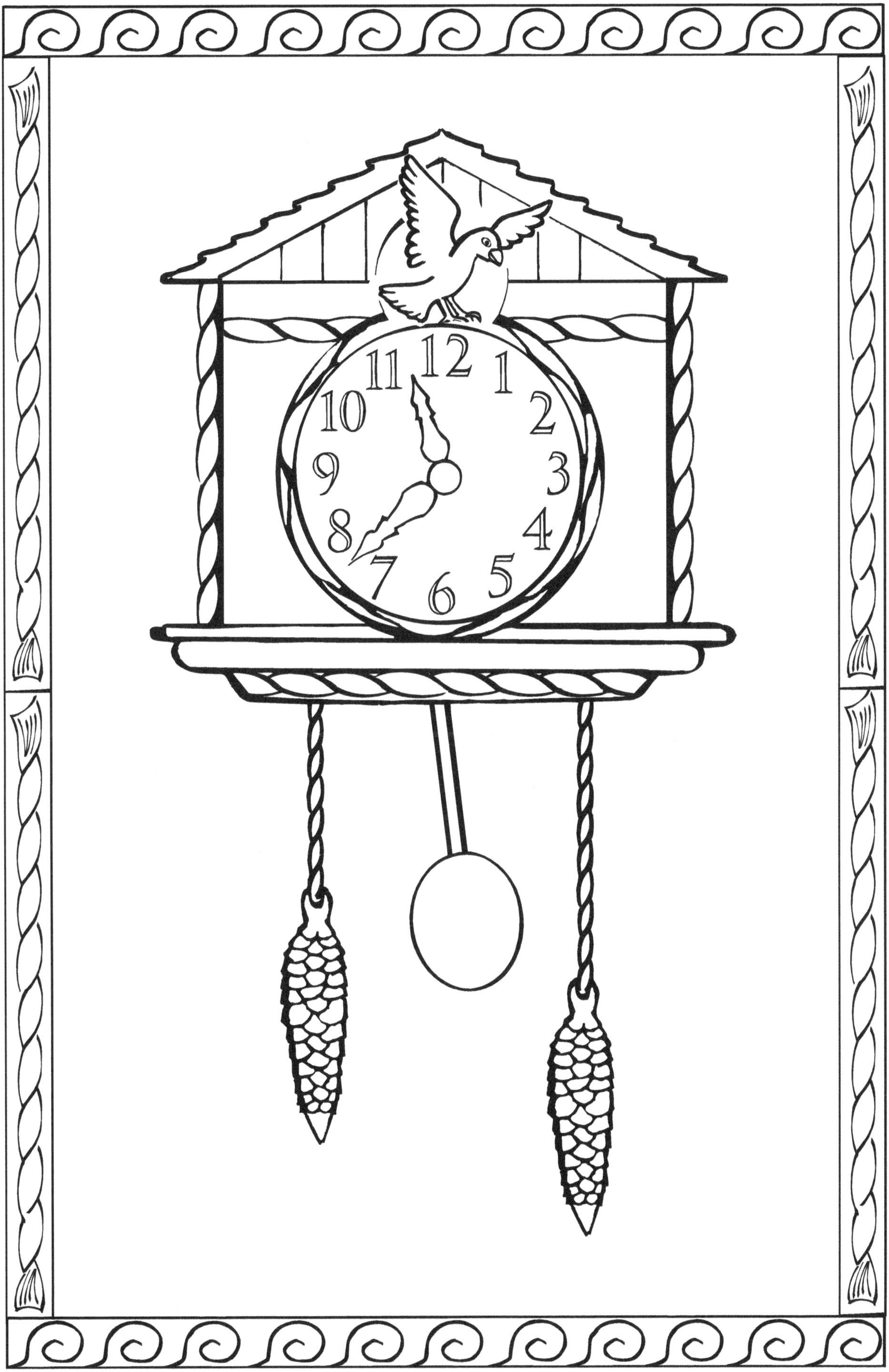
12
1
2
3
4
5
6
7
8
9
10
11

Henry walked up the stairs, went past his room, turned down a hallway, and opened a door. He then climbed up a narrow ladder that led to his secret place in the attic.

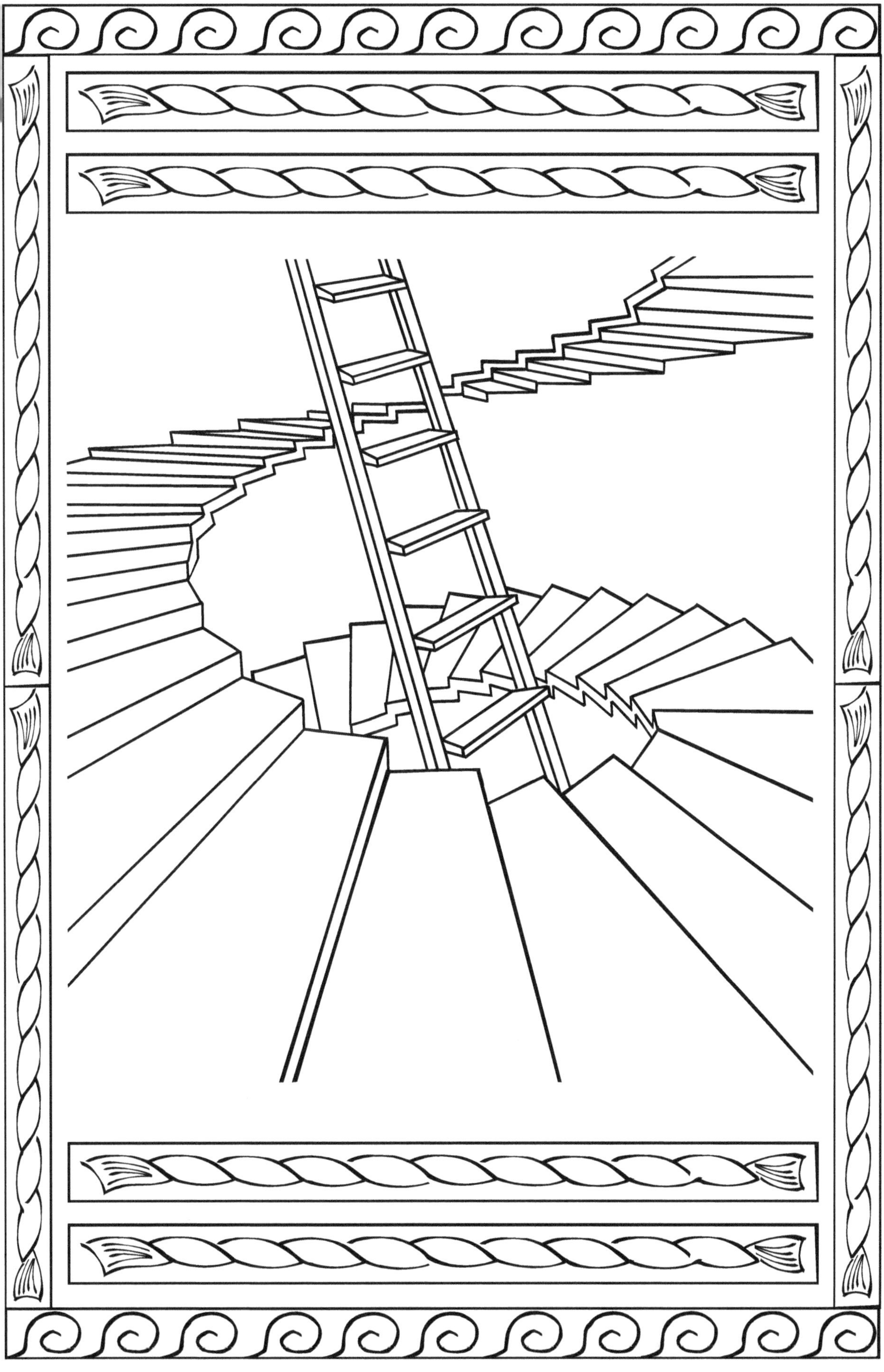

Here, he felt safe. He used to come to the attic with Daddy and help him at the work bench full of tools. They would spend hours sawing and hammering. They made new things or fixed broken things, like Henry's toys.

Now, the light was burned out over the work table. His father didn't do any work, not even at home.

Now, it was a barren place, except for a special corner that was his.

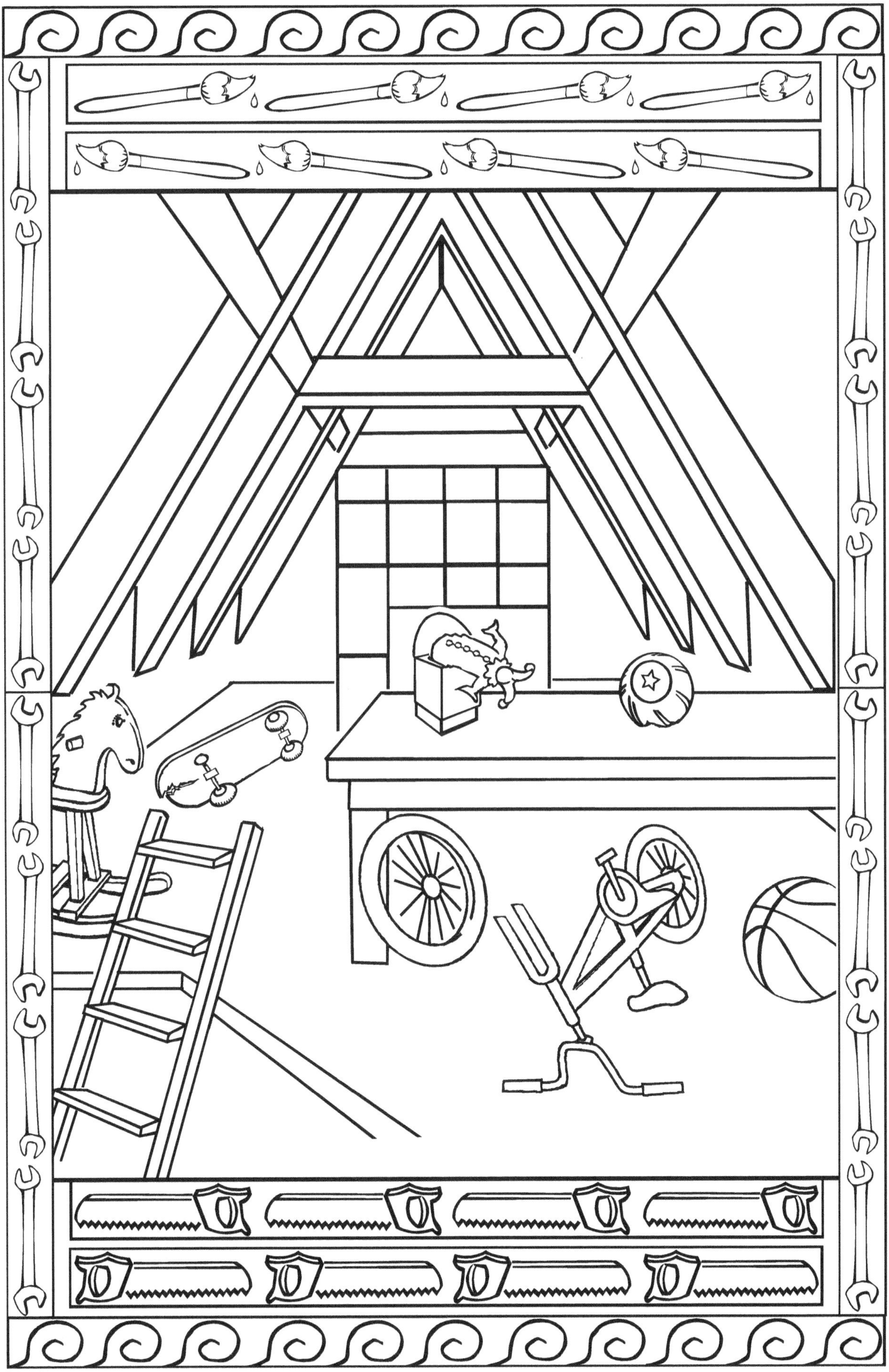

In Henry's corner, the light shined brightly.

He had a warm, cozy spot under the windows with a little rug, chair, cushions, Arthur the elephant, and Teddy, his oldest teddy bear that he'd loved the fur off of.

There were shelves for his books and a favorite picture he'd drawn on the wall.

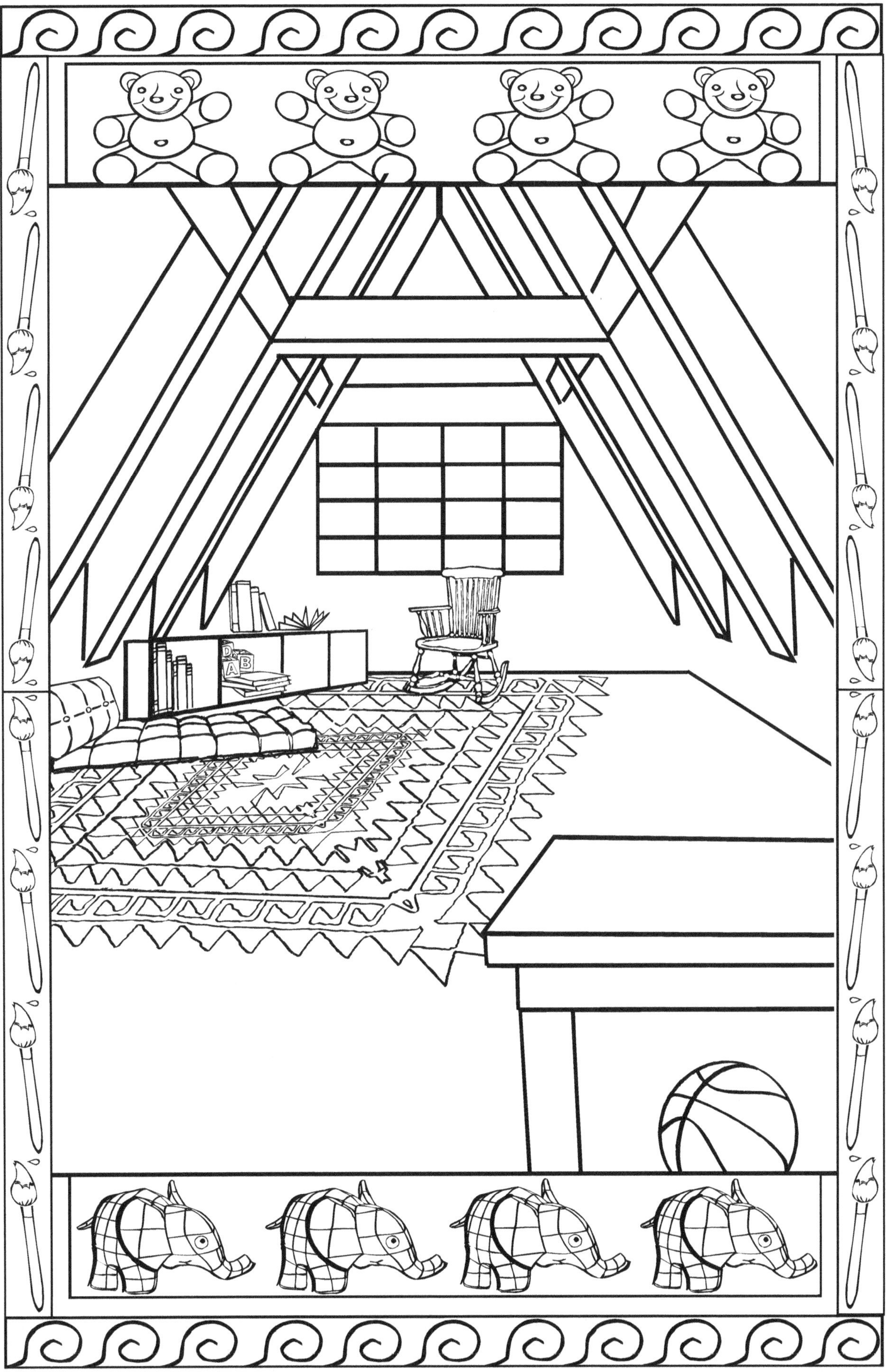
D
A
B

Henry made himself comfortable snuggling on the cushions with Teddy in some old blankets and watched the rain falling outside his window.

He thought about times before. Whenever he would fall and scrape or cut himself, Daddy used to give him licorice.

They would go on walks together through the woods, and often stop to get an ice cream on the way home.

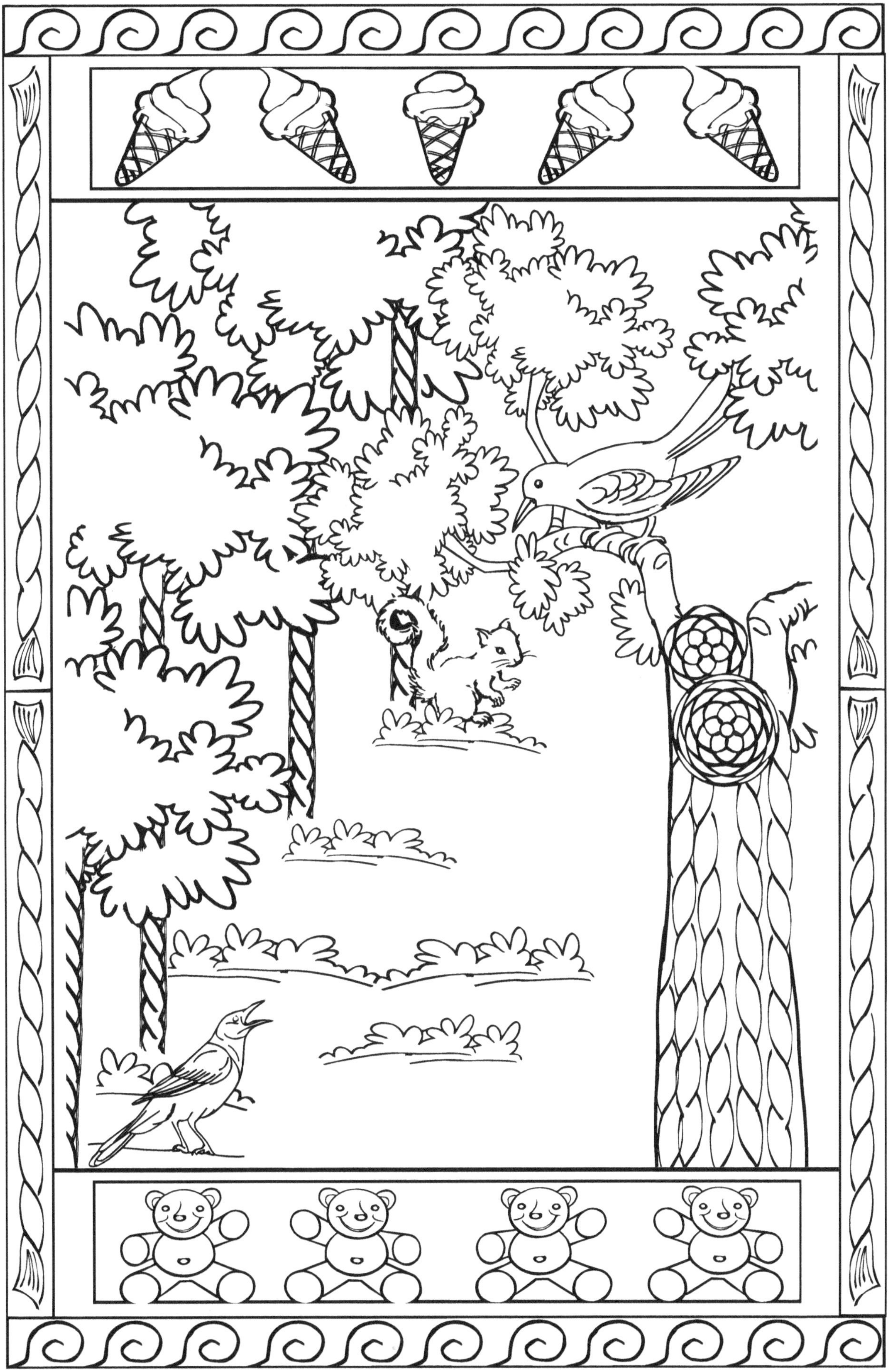

But tonight was different. His father was different than before. Tonight, the television had been on as usual during dinner time, the newscaster commenting about some war …

Instantly, Henry's father leaped up and turned off the TV. He made that strange grunting, almost a growling, sound.

When he sat back down, his face was red, his eyebrows close together. He looked mad, even mean. It frightened Henry.

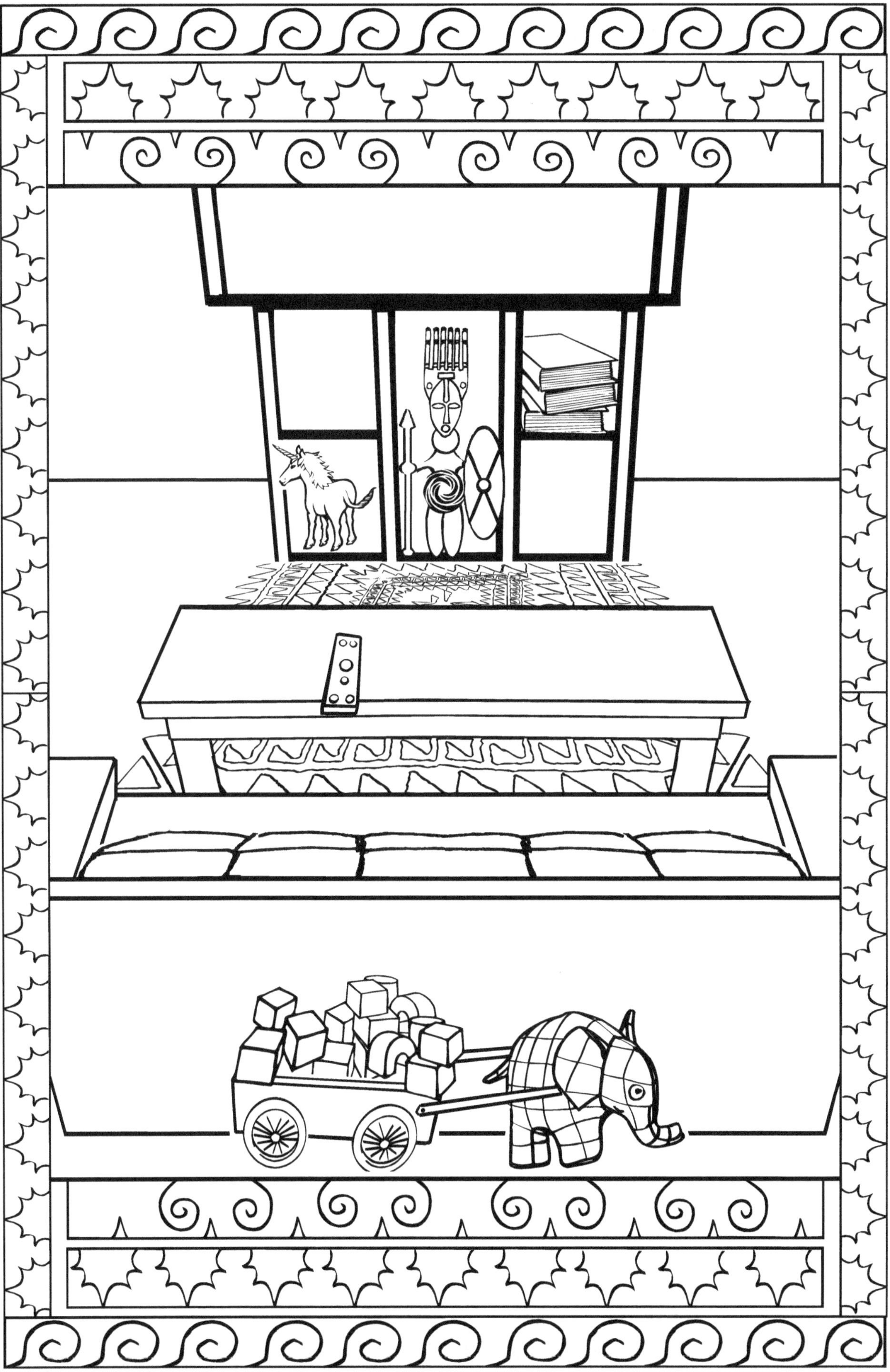

After dinner, right in the center of the living room, Henry built one of the tallest towers in the world.

Sitting down, he reached in his pocket and pulled out a stick of licorice. Chewing the licorice, he gazed at his creation and felt proud.

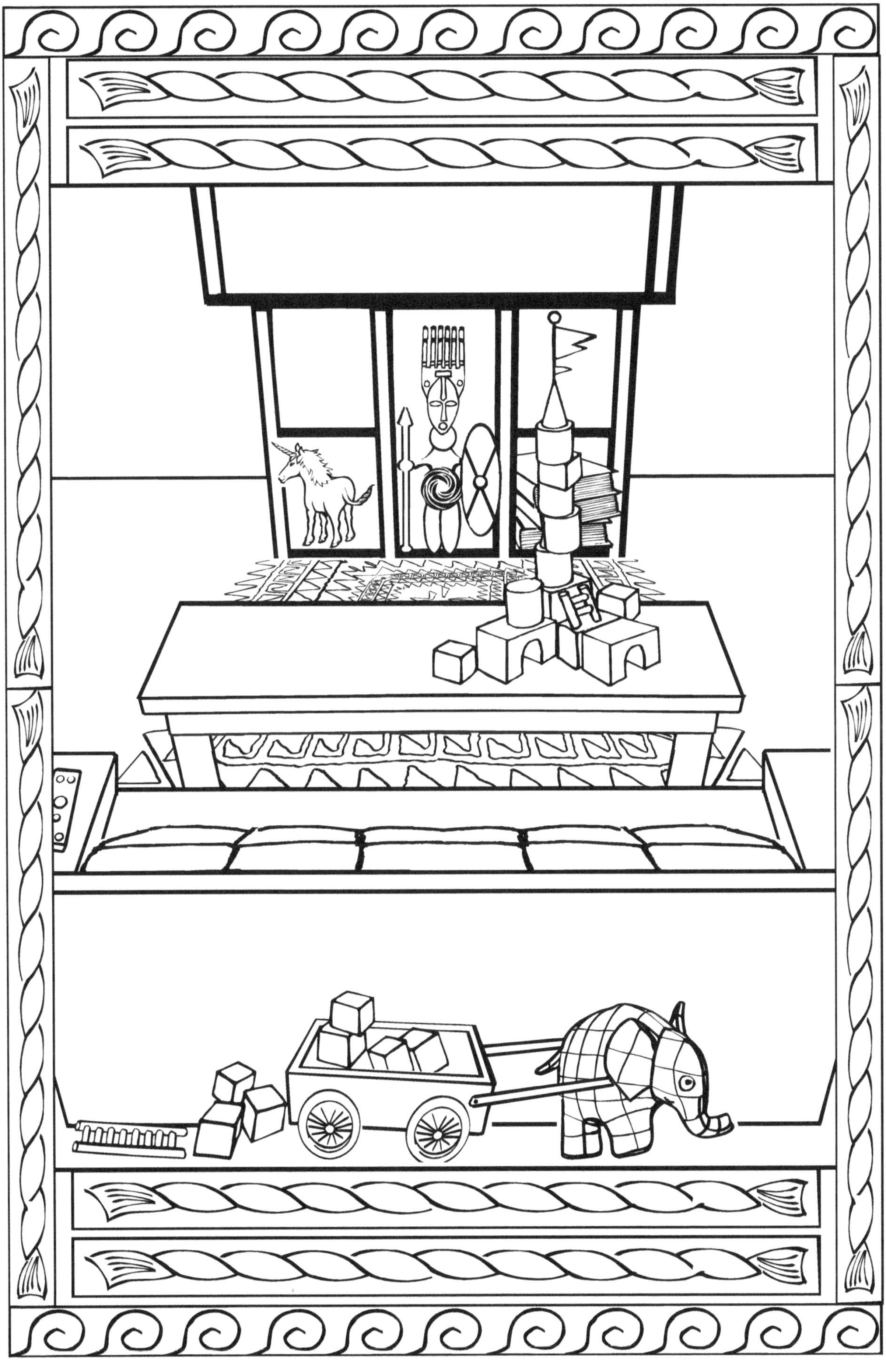

Suddenly, out of nowhere, his father stormed across the room. He knocked over Henry's tower. Henry was sad. Henry was angry.

Mama stood by helplessly.

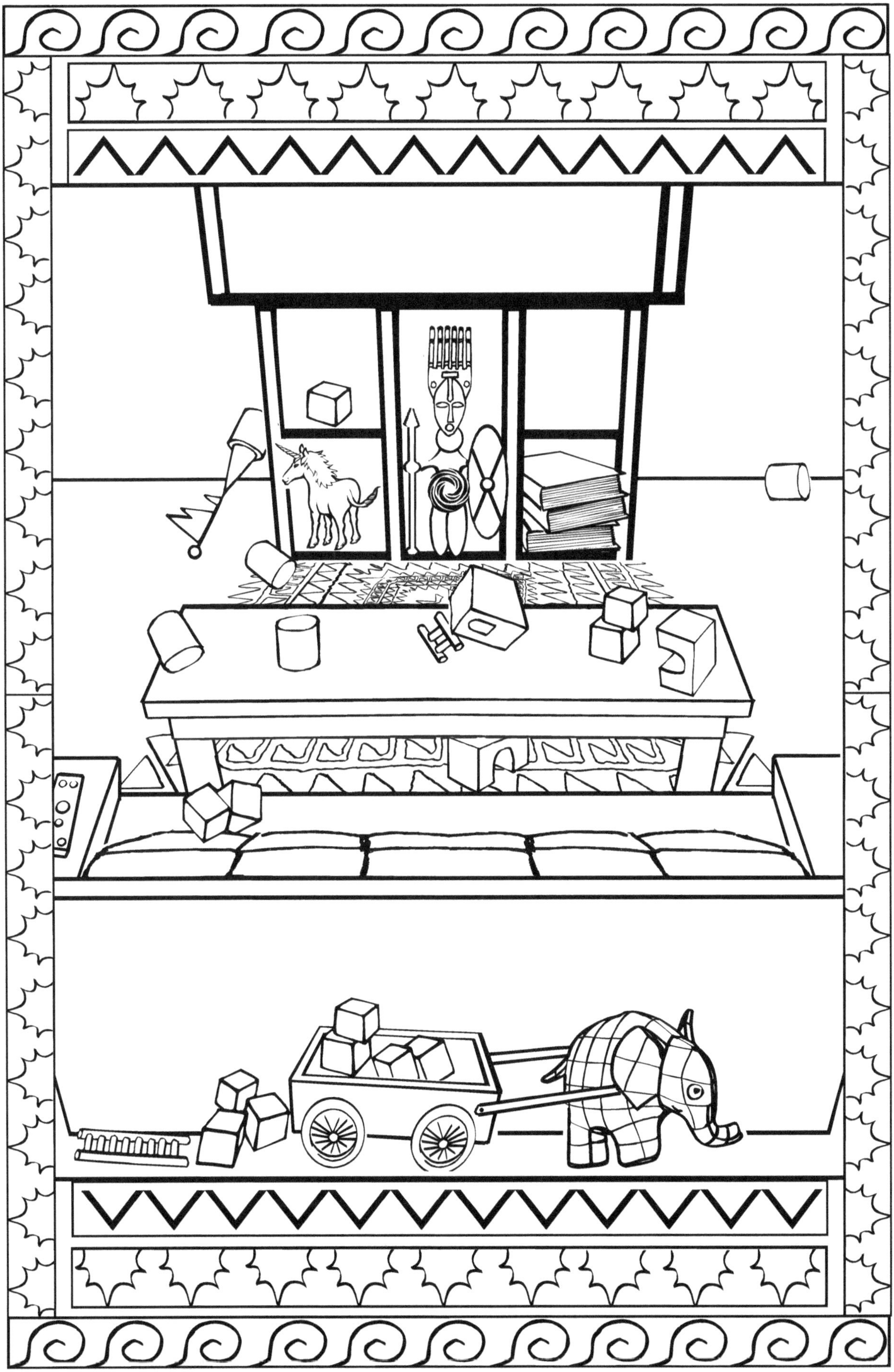

Henry, determined, rebuilt his tower.
He thought to himself, "This is the best
castle spire ever."

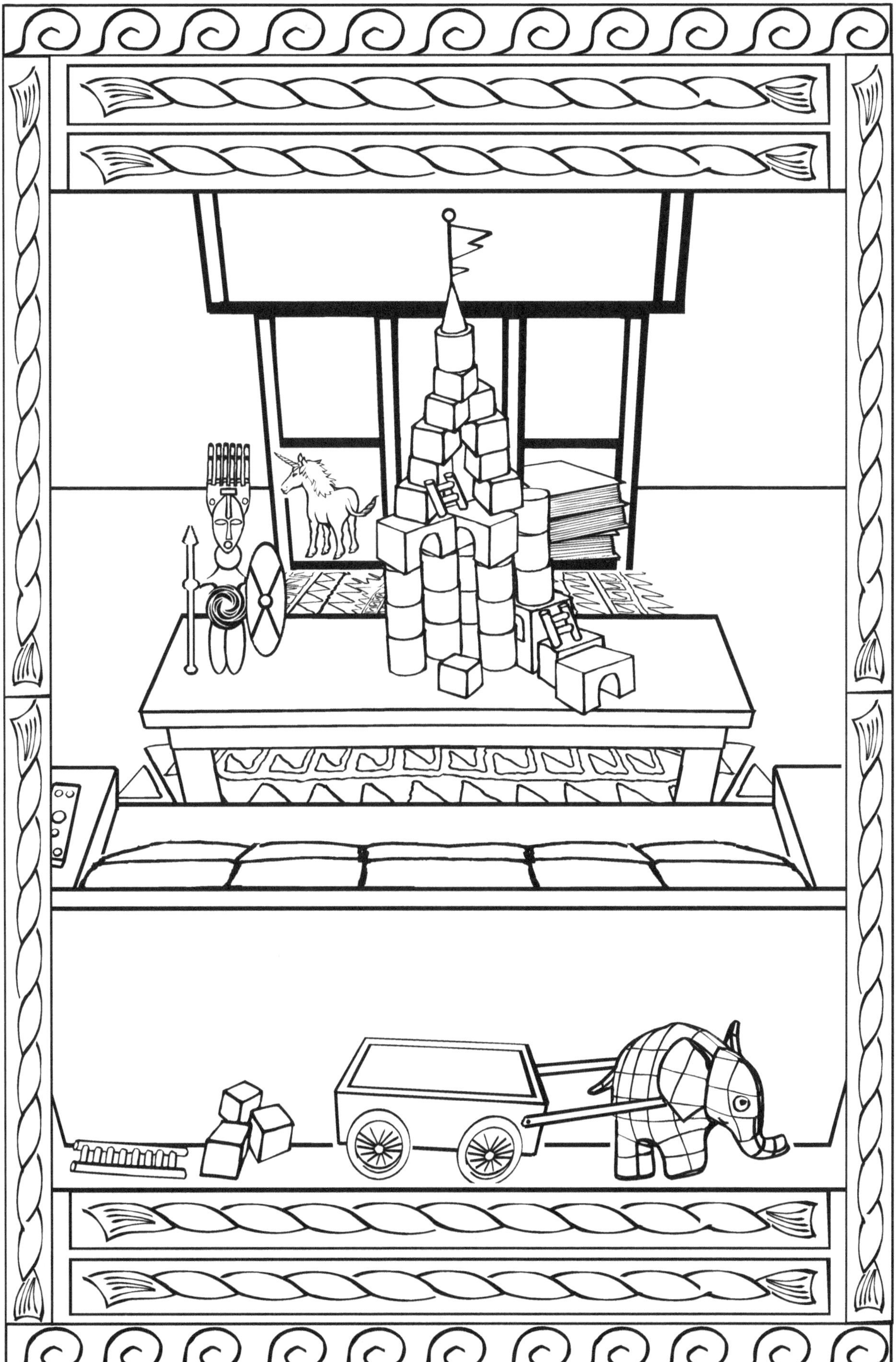

Then from the corner of his eye, he saw his father's rage coming his way.

Henry felt the back of his neck heating up. He started to tremble, and the palms of his hands were sweaty.

Henry felt like standing in front of his fortress, but he jumped back instead, screaming silently, "Don't knock it over!"

There was a great crashing of blocks. His tower was destroyed a second time.

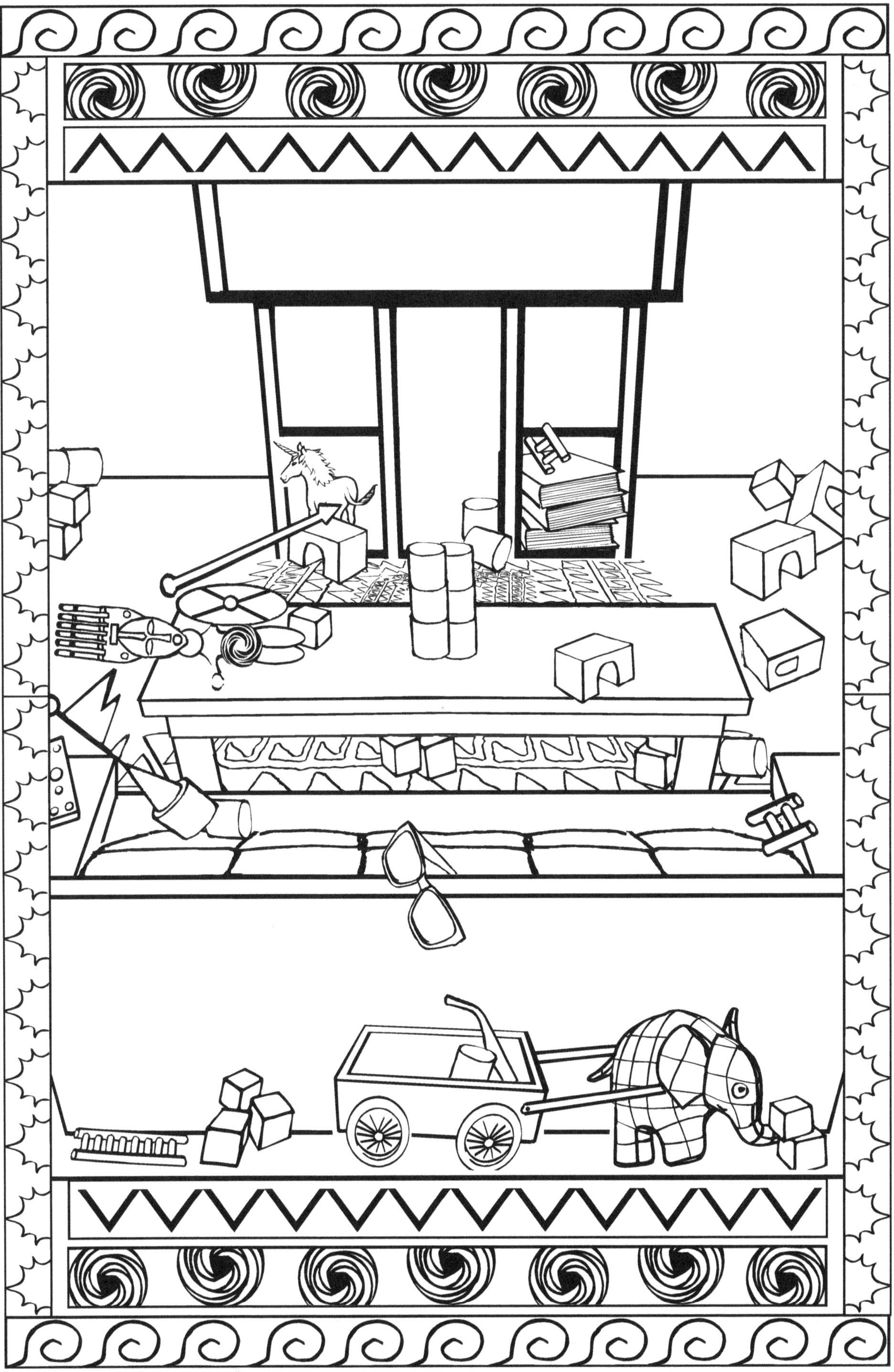

Henry was furious. With tears rolling down his cheeks, Henry picked up his blocks, dragging his block bag behind him.

Henry glared at his father who was sitting in a nook talking to the wall. As Henry stomped upstairs, he wondered why his father wasn't like he used to be. "We used to play baseball and fly kites!"

Last week, his father was going to take Henry and his two friends to a ball game.

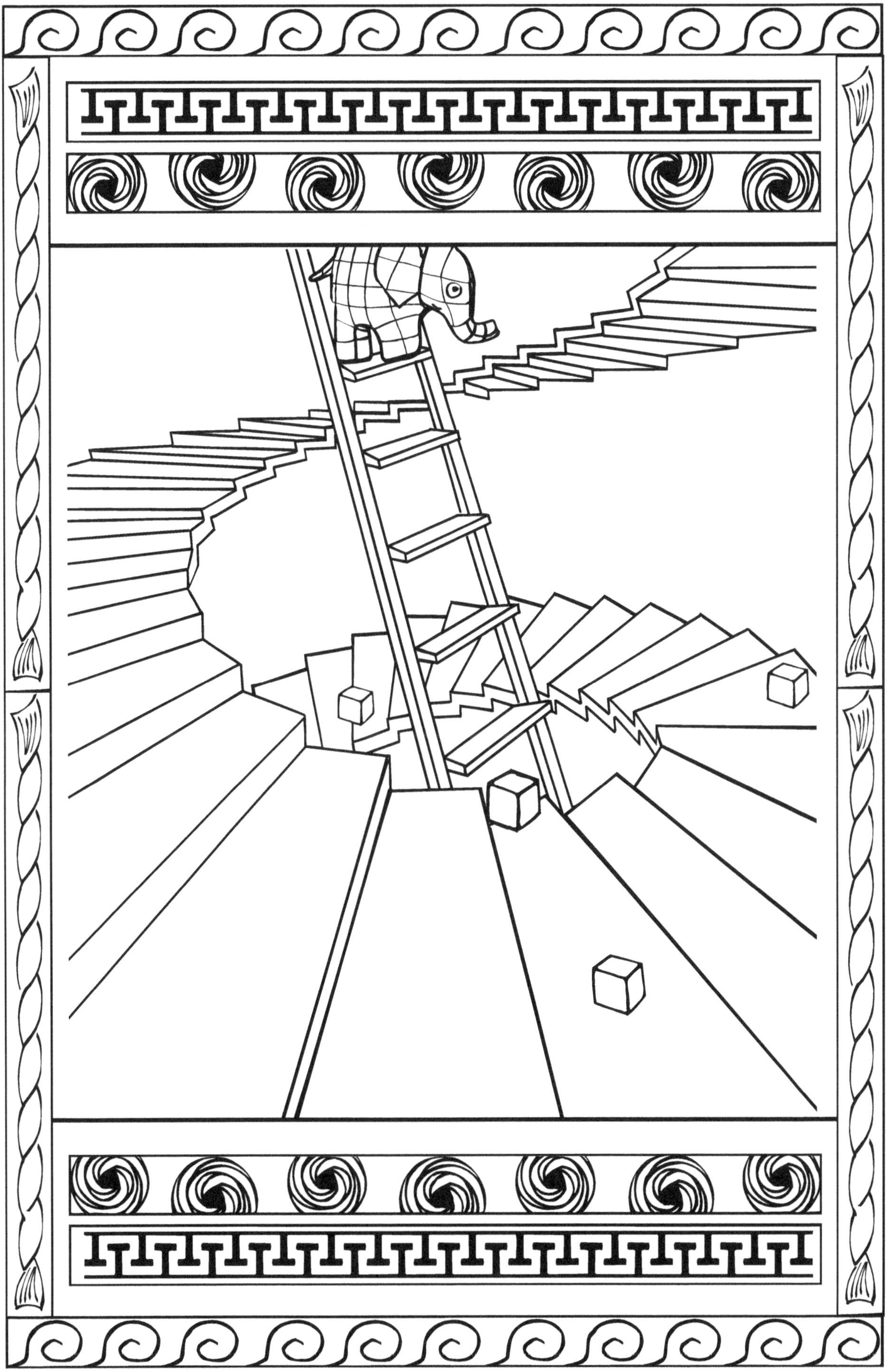

With that weird look in his eyes, his father arrived an hour late and started yelling at Henry, embarrassing him in front of his friends.

Henry ran home though the park. He was sure he'd get a spanking when he got home. But when he walked in the back door, Mama hugged him. She said with a sad voice, "It will be all right, Henry. Don't Worry."

His father was sitting down just staring out the front window.

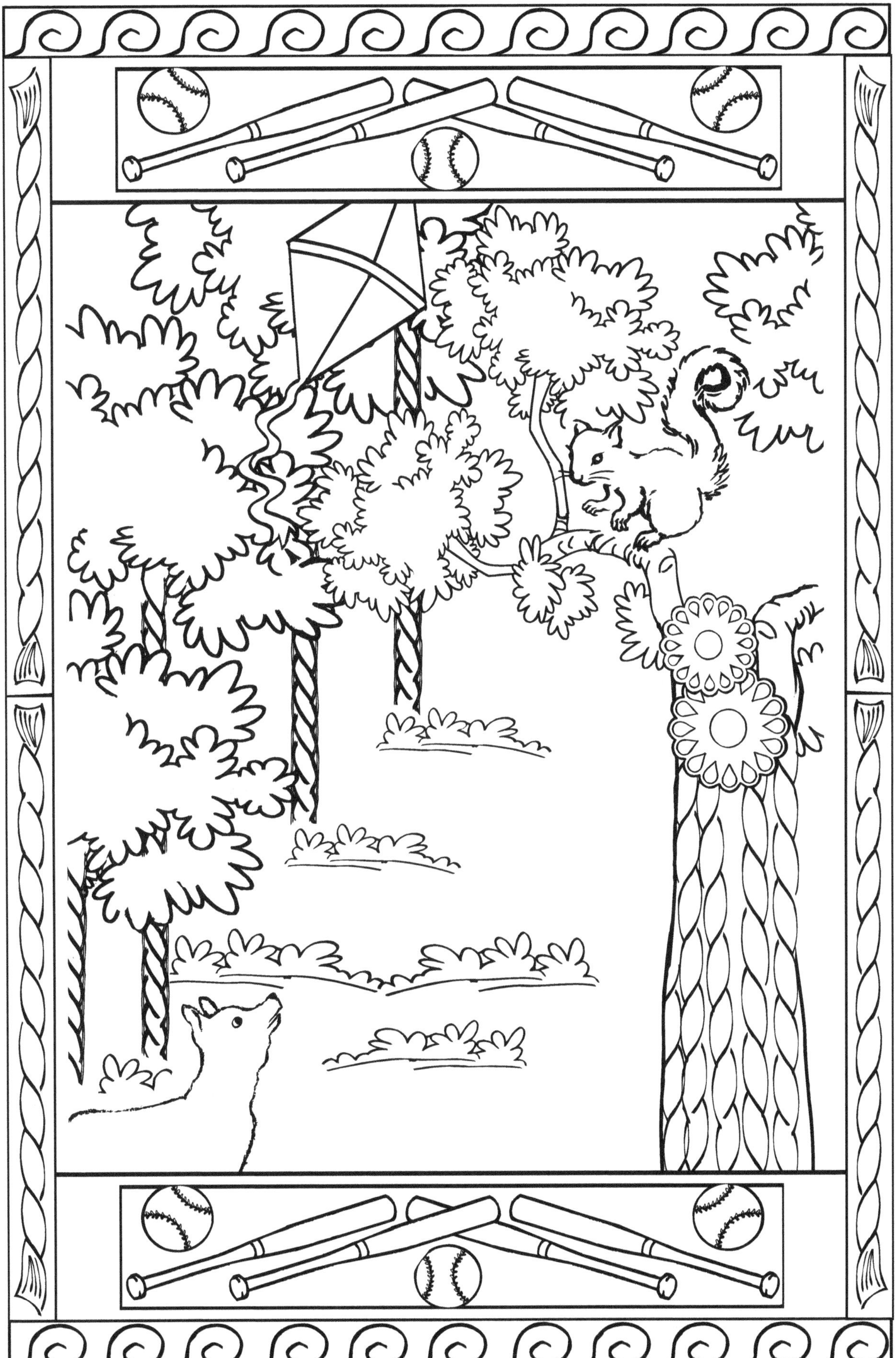

Now, in the attic, Henry had an idea. He combined the blocks he'd brought with him with ones he kept in his secret place. He began to construct another lofty tower. It became the highest and most beautiful one he had ever built.

Feeling much better, he curled up in his chair with one of his favorite books.

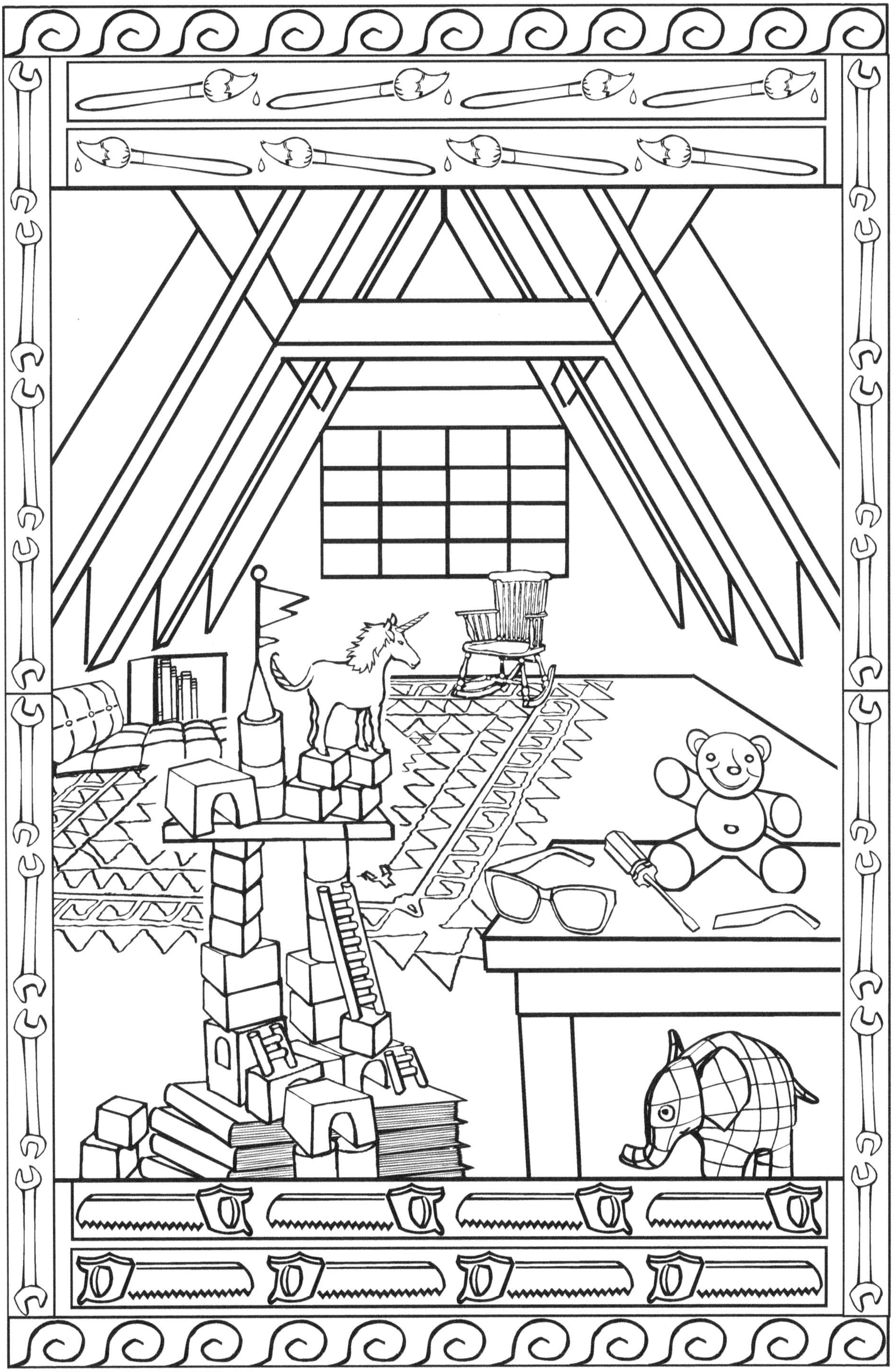

Henry was getting tired. Soon Mama called for him to come down for bed. When she was tucking him in, Henry asked, "What's wrong with Dad?"

Mama said, "I'm sorry about Daddy. I know it's hard Henry, but please try to understand. Your father is sick. His feelings were deeply hurt in the war."

"Will he get better?"

"I don't know, but I hope so. Like any hurt, it takes time to heal. It takes time and love." They both cried as Mama hugged and kissed him good night.

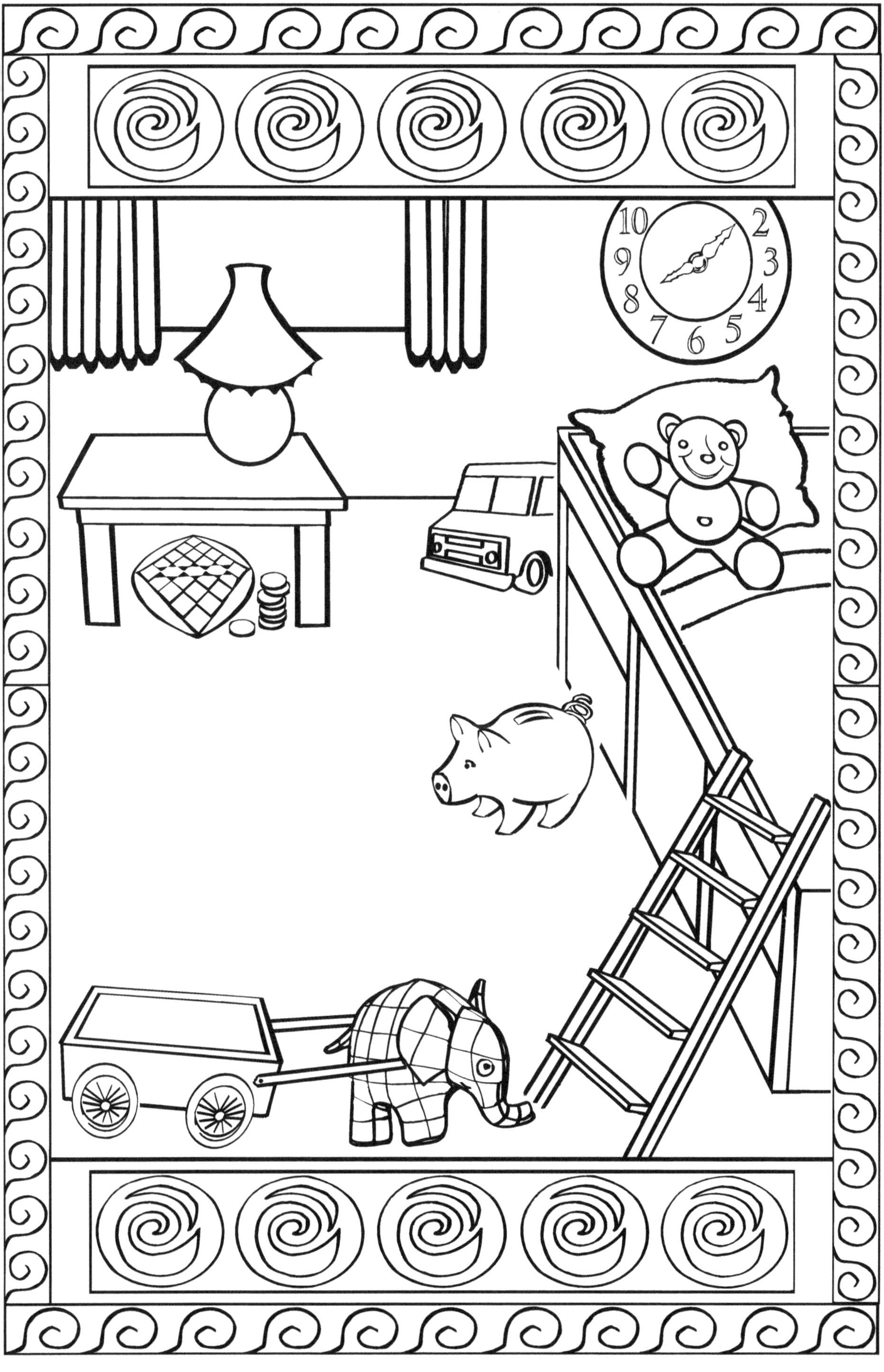

The next day, Henry didn't build a tower. Instead, he took eight coins out of his piggy bank and went to the store. He bought eight sticks of licorice.

When he got home, he quietly walked over to his father and gave him four licorice sticks. His father took these and looked at Henry fondly. Henry knew Daddy loved licorice as much as he did.

Henry thought to himself, "Time, love ... and licorice."

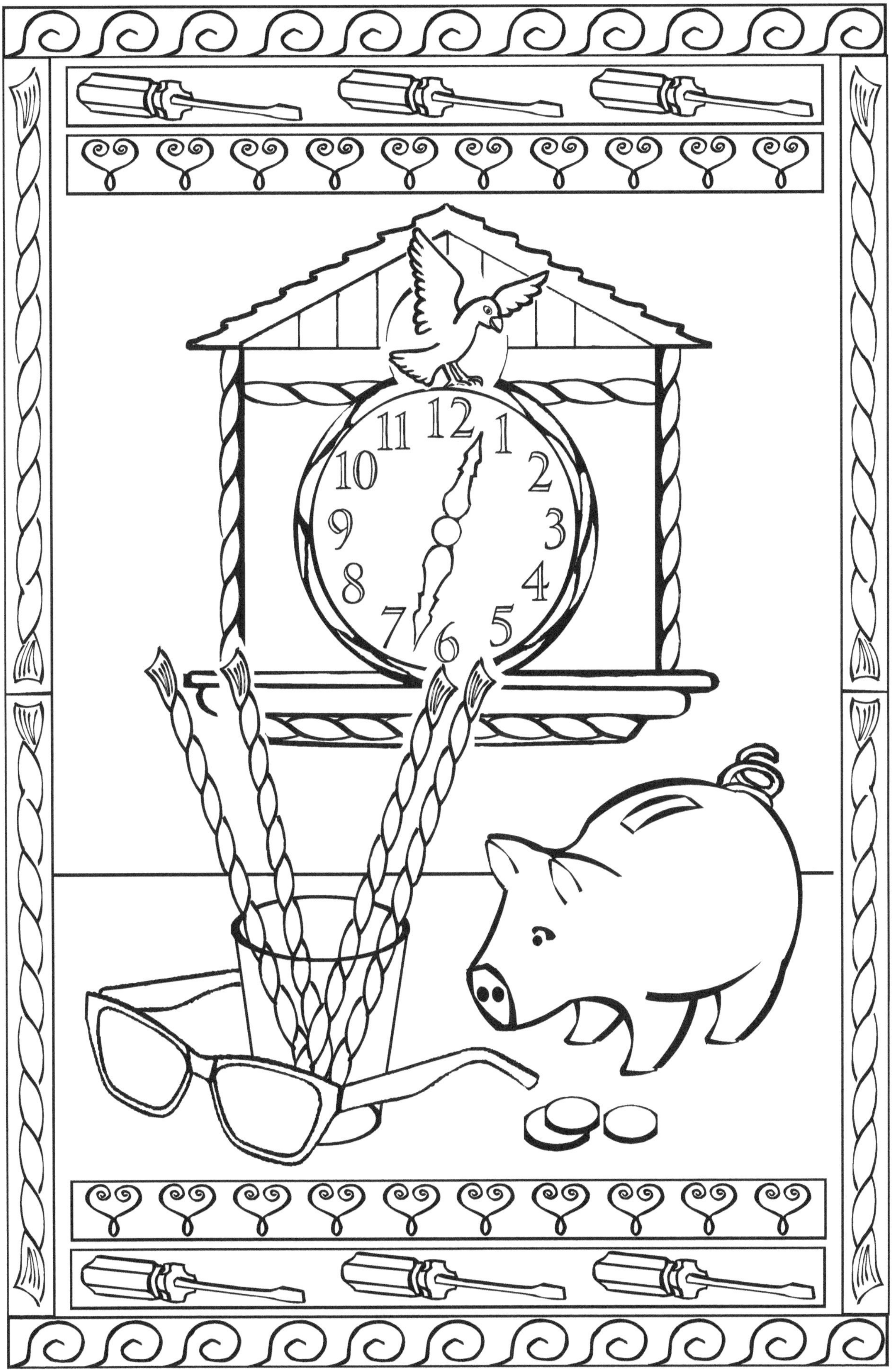
12
1
2
3
4
5
6
7
8
9
10
11

# ABOUT THE AUTHOR

Dr David H. Rosen is a physician, psychiatrist, and Jungian analyst. His interests include: finding meaning in suffering; spirituality as it relates to healing; dreams; and all kinds of creativity, especially visual art and haiku.

He is the author of eleven books, including *Transforming Depression: Healing the Soul through Creativity* (now in its third edition); *The Tao of Jung: The Way of Integrity*; *Medicine as Human Experience* with co-author Dr David Reiser, a classic in the field; *Lost in the Long White Cloud: Finding My Way Home*; *The Healing Spirit of Haiku* with co-author Joel Weishaus; and *The Tao of Elvis* from Rosenberry Books. Rosen's books have been translated into many languages.

David was born in 1945 in Port Chester, New York, and attended University of California, Berkeley and the University of Missouri School of Medicine. He received psychiatric training at the University of California, San Francisco and subsequent training in Jungian analysis. He was the initial holder of the McMillan Professorship in Analytical Psychology at Texas A&M University (the first of its kind in the world), and is now Affiliate Professor in Psychiatry at Oregon Health & Science University.

Currently living in Eugene, Oregon, with his wife Lanara and their rescued Akita named Suki, David walks, paints, sees analytic patients, and leads a dream group.

---

## ALSO OF INTEREST FROM ROSENBERRY BOOKS:
800.723.0336

*The Tao of Elvis*, David H. Rosen, MD, illus. Diane Katz

"Magnificent ... Truly a work of art. It brings to mind the inspired illuminated manuscripts of the Middle Ages." — Sue Monk Kidd, author of *The Secret Life of Bees*. In a most readable fashion, Rosen illuminates the inner Elvis and the myth of Elvis. Sumptuously designed and illlustrated.

*Words & Swords: a series of journaling journeys with Bernie*, Bernie Siegel, MD

Here is your chance to sit down with Bernie and write! Each of Bernie's poems is paired with the space for you to express your feelings and thoughts — providing an opportunity for healing & growth ... and to laugh a little with Bernie!

Spritual-health teacher Bernie Siegel is the author of many popular self-help

# ABOUT THE ARTIST

Diane has seen the value of emotional transformation through artistic expression. She uses a high-energy, emotion-releasing technique to draw with creamy blocks of beeswax crayons. The result is a cross between printing, drawing and monument rubbing, in which hidden images magically reveal themselves on the surface of the paper.

This technique was used to create the cover of *Time, Love and Licorice,* as well as Diane's illustrations for *Beneath the Willow Tree, Garden Snippets* and *Apples Dipped in Honey: A Jewish ABC.*

Other healing books that include Diane's artwork are: *Purple: A Parable* (for children & adults); *The Tao of Elvis* by Dr Rosen; *On All My Holy Mountain*: *A Modern Fraktur* (for families); and *The Story-Letters from Appletta Tooth Fairy.*

Through Rosenberry Books, Diane's work has been seen at the Metropolitan Museum of Art, the Smithsonian, the Chicago Institute of Art, Washington National Cathedral, etc. and recognized by Design Observer of the Winterhouse Institute.

Diane lives with her husband in the woods of North Carolina among the fox squirrels, rabbits, deer, and green anole lizards. Interested in the curative properties of herbs, she is delighted to discover that candy made from real licorice root can be used to help heal adrenal exhaustion and stress.

books, including *Love, Medicine & Miracles; Faith, Hope & Healing;* and for healthy parenting, *Love, Magic & Mud Pies.*

*Purple: A Parable* by Alexis Rotella, illus. Diane Katz

Can creative truth survive in the face of childhood cruelty? Bernie Siegel, MD says,"Purple touches the heart of everyone I read it to, and it has become a part of my lectures. Purple speaks the essential message to all of us..."

When Mrs Lohr assigned a teepee drawing, the child responds with a joyous vision of horses, a grinning sun and purple-patterned teepee. Mrs Lohr rejected the drawing saying "purple was a color for people who died." We watch the joyous vision die with the child's efforts to do as she was told. What remains of creativity is expressed in the child's formless gray doodles which creep about the edges of school writing paper. Until wise Mr Barta's 2nd-grade class...

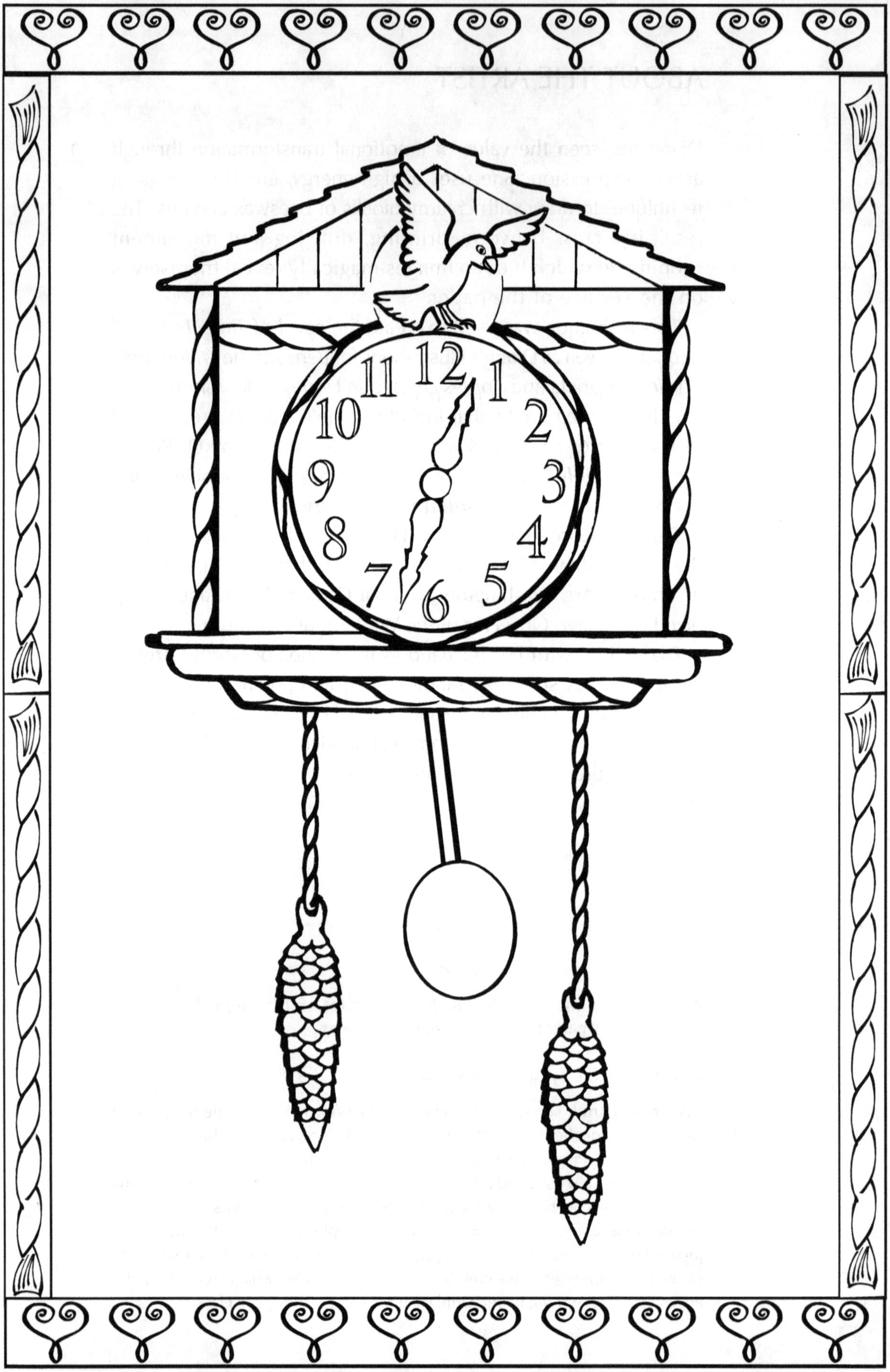
12
1
2
3
4
5
6
7
8
9
10
11

www.ingramcontent.com/pod-product-compliance
Lightning Source LLC
Chambersburg PA
CBHW081423270326
41931CB00015B/3384